COLLE

Titles in Dark Reads:

Blood Moon
Barbara Catchpole

Doctor Jekyll and Little Miss Hyde
Tony Lee

Red Handed
Ann Evans

Ringtone
Tommy Donbavand

Ship of the Dead
Alex Woolf

Straw Men
Ann Evans

The Black-Eyed Girl
Tim Collins

The Girl in the Wall
Tommy Donbavand

Badger Publishing Limited, Oldmedow Road, Hardwick Industrial Estate, King's Lynn PE30 4JJ
Telephone: 01438 791037

www.badgerlearning.co.uk

TOMMY DONBAVAND

Ringtone ISBN 978-1-78464-085-9

Text © Tommy Donbavand 2015
Complete work © Badger Publishing Limited 2015

Publisher: Susan Ross
Senior Editor: Danny Pearson
Publishing Assistant: Claire Morgan
Copyeditor: Cheryl Lanyon
Designer: Bigtop Design Ltd
Illustrator: Mark Penman

2 4 6 8 10 9 7 5 3 1

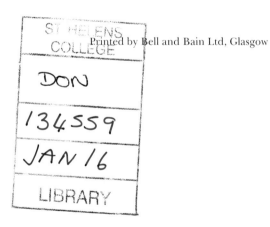
Printed by Bell and Bain Ltd, Glasgow

CHAPTER 1
THE TREE

I didn't mean to kill Ben. He was my
best friend…

We did everything together. We even had a special ringtone on our phones for when we called each other. It was us singing our favourite rock song.

That day, we bunked off maths and went to the woods.

"You're too chicken to climb to the top of that tree!" I shouted.

"No, I'm not!" he shouted back.

So Ben climbed higher and higher, and I started to shake the branches. Just to scare him a bit. But he slipped and fell. He hit the ground hard and banged his head on a rock. There was blood everywhere.

"Ben?" I said.

He didn't reply.

CHAPTER 2
THE PHONE CALL

Ben had no pulse. My best friend was dead. I had killed him.

I was scared. What if I was sent to prison for murder?

I had to hide Ben's body. I dug a hole in the earth with my hands and dragged him in.

I covered him up with soil and leaves.

I ran home, trying not to think about what I had done.

"Where's Ben?" asked mum. "You said he was coming for tea tonight."

"He changed his mind," I said. "We don't do everything together, you know!"

I ran up to my room and slammed the door. I lay on my bed and cried.

Then my phone began to ring – with our special ringtone!

CHAPTER 3

THE WHISPER

I picked up my phone.

If that ringtone was playing, there was only one person who could be calling.

Ben!

"Hello?"

All I could hear was wind howling and leaves rustling. The sound of the woods.

I went to the window and looked out. Could Ben be out there, watching me?

No, I had checked his pulse. He was dead.

Then I heard his voice on the phone.
It sounded like a whisper.

"Why did you do it, Darren?" he asked.
"Why did you kill me?"

"I... I didn't mean it!" I said. "It was
an accident!"

I quickly pulled the back off my phone and took out the battery.

Now I wouldn't have to hear my friend saying I had killed him again.

CHAPTER 4

THE LIE

Ben's dad came round later that night.

"Do you know where Ben might be?"
he asked.

I thought of Ben, lying in the grave I had
dug in the woods. "No," I lied.

Then Ben's dad's phone began to ring.
He had put it on the coffee table with his
car keys.

I stared down at it in horror. It was playing
our ringtone.

"Are you going to answer that?" I asked.

"Answer what?" said Ben's dad.

"Your phone," I said.

"My phone's not ringing," said Ben's dad.

That wasn't true. His phone was ringing. Why couldn't he hear it?

I grabbed the phone. "Hello?" I said.

"Why did you kill me?" whispered Ben.

I dropped the phone and ran upstairs to bed, but I couldn't sleep.

CHAPTER 5

THE TRUTH

The next day, I was called to the head teacher's office to speak to a police officer.

"We know that you and Ben bunked off yesterday," the policewoman said. "Where did you go?"

Before I could answer, the policewoman's radio hissed and crackled with the sound of me and Ben singing our favourite rock song. Our ringtone. But the adults didn't pay it any attention. They couldn't hear it.

"Tell them, Darren…" whispered Ben's voice on the radio. "Tell them what you did to me…"

He was never going to leave me alone. I didn't have a choice. So I took a deep breath.

"I didn't mean to kill Ben," I said. "He was my best friend…"

STORY FACTS

My inspiration for writing this story was *The Tell-Tale Heart* by Edgar Allan Poe.

First published in 1843, this short story is about the gruesome murder of an old man.

The murderer buries the old man's body beneath the floorboards of his house.

But he believes he can still hear his heart beating.

The sound gradually drives him insane.

Finally, he confesses to the police and tells them where to find the body.

Tommy Donbavand

QUESTIONS

Where did Darren and Ben go?
(page 6)

What did Darren's mum ask about Ben?
(page 12)

Who did Darren think was calling him?
(page 14)

What did the voice on the phone say to Darren?
(page 18)

Who came to speak to Darren at school?
(page 26)

Who wrote the story *The Tell-Tale Heart*?
(page 30)

MEET THE AUTHOR

Tommy Donbavand has written over 60 books for children. Most of them are so scary that you have to sleep with the lights on after reading them! His 13-book *Scream Street* series is being made for TV now. Recently, he wrote his first Doctor Who novel, *Shroud of Sorrow*. Tommy lives in Lancashire with his wife, two sons and more and more pets!

MEET THE ARTIST

Mark Penman thinks he maybe played one too many fantasy games (on his computer). Now it seems he can only silence the terrifying voices in his head by drawing scary stories starring terrified teens.